HAL LEONARD

LAP SLIDE SONGBOOK

Play Solo Slide Guitar Arrangements of
22 Country, Folk, Blues and Rock Songs

BY PETER ROLLER

AUDIO ACCESS INCLUDED

PLAYBACK+
Speed • Pitch • Balance • Loop

To access audio visit:
www.halleonard.com/mylibrary

Enter Code
6151-8586-3111-3479

ISBN 978-1-5400-2269-1

Visit Hal Leonard Online at
www.halleonard.com

Contact us:
Hal Leonard
7777 West Bluemound Road
Milwaukee, WI 53213
Email: info@halleonard.com

In Europe, contact:
Hal Leonard Europe Limited
42 Wigmore Street
Marylebone, London, W1U 2RN
Email: info@halleonardeurope.com

In Australia, contact:
Hal Leonard Australia Pty. Ltd.
4 Lentara Court
Cheltenham, Victoria, 3192 Australia
Email: info@halleonard.com.au

CONTENTS

4   Introduction

5   Song Notes

8   You Gotta Move — FRED MCDOWELL

9   No Expectations — THE ROLLING STONES

10 My Babe — LITTLE WALTER

12 Outside Woman Blues — CREAM

14 John Henry — FOLK SONG

16 The Soul of a Man — BLIND WILLIE JOHNSON

17 The Great Speckled Bird — ROY ACUFF

18 You Are My Sunshine — VARIOUS

20 Shenandoah — FOLK SONG

22 Cripple Creek — FIDDLE TUNE

24 Red Wing — FIDDLE TUNE

26 The Red Haired Boy — FIDDLE TUNE

27 Angelina Baker — STEPHEN FOSTER

29 Lonesome Fiddle Blues — VASSAR CLEMENTS

30 Gold Rush — BILL MONROE

32 Fireball — FOGGY MOUNTAIN BOYS

34 Poor Boy, Long Ways from Home — TRADITIONAL

35 Steamboat Gwine 'Round de Bend — JOHN FAHEY

38 Come on in My Kitchen — ROBERT JOHNSON

40 Dark Was the Night, Cold Was the Ground — BLIND WILLIE JOHNSON

42 (Sittin' On) The Dock of the Bay — OTIS REDDING

44 Little Martha — THE ALLMAN BROTHERS BAND

47 Lap Slide Notation Legend

INTRODUCTION

Playing slide on an acoustic guitar held on the lap has a soulfulness felt by both musician and listeners. For roots of the approach, most attention has been given to Hawaiian guitarists who pioneered playing lap-style with a small piece of steel (a derivation of the term "steel guitar"), however, African-American blues and gospel musicians in the South alternated upright bottleneck with the lap slide approach in their own music during the same early-twentieth-century time period. This songbook features early country music strongly influenced by first-generation Hawaiian steel guitarists, later bluegrass Dobro tunes, African-American blues and spirituals, as well as arrangements of more recent fingerstyle, rock, and soul songs that are suited to lap slide.

The book is arranged in stylistic sections, allowing the learner to move from beginning-level to advanced-intermediate playing in each genre. The final section has an eclectic mix of advanced-level lap slide solos. It is advised that guitarists first gain confidence in playing earlier pieces in the book to possess the fundamental techniques needed to learn the more advanced music.

Use the accompanying recorded examples to get the basic tune in your head and don't be afraid to seek out the original versions of songs as played by master guitarists. Most importantly, have both patience in learning new playing styles and fun in trying to eventually do your own thing—none of this lap slide music is set in stone!

Photo: Brian Malloy

Peter Roller

Note on guitars, slides (steels), and picks: A steel-string acoustic guitar with high action can be used to try most of the music in this book, however a resonator guitar with a strong square neck is advised for the country and bluegrass Dobro tunes since the "high bass" G tuning puts great stress on a standard guitar neck, and the resonator tone is strongly associated with these styles. As to steels, guitarists can use a metal slide with thick walls for decent tone, preferable is a Stevens steel-type solid bar that has flanges for easy holding and the weight for superior tone.

The blues, spirituals, fingerstyle, rock, and soul songs in this book can be fingerpicked with bare fingers (or thumbpick and fingers), however the Dobro tunes are played with a thumb and two fingerpicks.

SONG NOTES

Beginning to Intermediate Blues, Spirituals & Rock Songs

Like so many others, I first heard acoustic and electric slide playing through Rolling Stones records, but not knowing anything about this approach I held an acoustic guitar in open tuning on my lap and used a glass tumbler from the kitchen as a slide! For the Fred McDowell slide spiritual "You Gotta Move" (covered by the Stones), first learn the treble melody with plenty of vibrato on held notes and then add the answering bass riff. For "No Expectations," play slowly on this country-flavored song with the long slides dragged out!

The song "My Babe" is arranged for lap slide based on Fred McDowell's bottleneck version. As with his previous song, give plenty of vibrato to held notes and work on muting the quickly strummed open-string chords using the pinky of your hand holding the steel or slide.

"Outside Woman Blues" is a lap slide version of Blind Joe Reynold's original recording from the 1920s that inspired Eric Clapton with Cream's version in the late 1960s. This is the book's first lap slide arrangement with a high degree of syncopation between the treble melody, representing the blues vocal, and the steady bass pattern. Learn the melody parts before adding the bass!

Found in both African-American and country music traditions, "John Henry" is the first songbook tune arranged with alternating bass accompaniment in open G tuning. Note that in the 12th and 16th measures, an E minor chord is sounded briefly by covering the bottom three strings (only) with the steel at the second fret. Take time to get used to alternating this with melody notes played on higher strings where the bar is tipped up.

"The Soul of a Man" is a spiritual song originated by Blind Willie Johnson and covered most notably by David Lindley (versions on both Arabic oud and Weisenborn lap slide). This arrangement features a syncopated riff played before each verse/chorus section of the song. Spend time mastering the tricky riff before giving attention to the song melody with its many slides and embellishments!

Beginning to Intermediate Country & Bluegrass Dobro

Dobro slow songs frequently played in old-time country and bluegrass music, "You Are My Sunshine" and "Great Speckled Bird," require the lap slide guitarist to learn two-note harmony playing and slants with the steel. Try the familiar "Sunshine" tune in harmony, but feel free to repeatedly drill the couple of slants to get used to quickly moving the bar (while staying somewhat in tune!). "Great Speckled Bird" is a universal melody also heard in the country songs "I'm Thinking Tonight of My Blue Eyes" and "The Wild Side of Life" (three tunes in one!). Take time to learn the slants on the 1st and 3rd strings—an approach found in many early Hawaiian steel guitar pieces.

The classic American folksong "Shenandoah" has both a harmony version, featuring a few slants, and an additional arrangement in octaves where the bar is held straight throughout. Playing lap slide melodies in octaves is frequently found in both country and blues styles.

The fiddle tunes "Cripple Creek," "Red Wing," and "The Red Haired Boy" are often played in bluegrass circles. Start slow and then move to a faster tempo with each one and get used to moving the tipped bar quickly in playing these fast-moving melodies!

The two Dobro songs "Angelina Baker" and "Lonesome Fiddle Blues" offer melodies in the key of D while in the traditional, high-bass open G tuning. "Angelina Baker" is the simplest tune in the book (the song's chorus simply states the beloved Angelina's name over and over), so I offer a second, harmony version played "up the neck" that combines open and fretted notes for a challenge! "Lonesome Fiddle Blues," originated by the great fiddler Vassar Clements and played by current bluegrass jam bands, allows us to learn a minor-key melody played in the "bar bouncing" style of Jerry Douglas. Memorize the tune at a slower tempo and then increase to warp speed!

Fast bluegrass breakdowns like mandolinist Bill Monroe's "Gold Rush" and Dobroist Josh Graves' "Fireball" require repeated playing to acquire the fast bar movement and picking needed. Note that "Fireball" has a contrasting B section with slower-moving, bluesy slides that should be dragged out compared to the banjo rolls (imitating Earl Scruggs) found in the A section!

Advanced-Level Lap Slide Solos

Memphis Jug Band musician Gus Cannon played his version of the early blues standard "Poor Boy, Long Ways from Home" with a slide on banjo, where the small body allowed access to very high frets. Played on lap slide, we can imitate Cannon's high riff in a way not easily done on upright bottleneck guitar! Practice the repeating riff until it's memorized so you can easily insert it between phrases of this blues song. Be conscious of keeping the slide extended so it only covers the first few strings, leaving bass notes open, a technique frequently found in the following tunes.

"Steamboat 'Gwine Round de Bend" was John Fahey's signature lap slide piece, played on a Weisenborn squareneck lap guitar as a change from his many fingerstyle acoustic guitar pieces. (It is also the lead song on his Warner Brothers album *Of Rivers and Religion*). Keep a slow, steady muted bass accompaniment throughout this long piece that features many slight variations.

"Come on in My Kitchen" is Robert Johnson's masterpiece bottleneck slow song. This lap slide arrangement will call on your earlier learning of keeping the bar extended only over treble strings (with open bass notes) and combining a highly syncopated vocal melody with a steady "thunk" bass. Listen to the amazing performance in Robert's original recording of the song (his first take, slow version of "Come on in My Kitchen").

"Dark Was the Night, Cold Was the Ground" is Blind Willie Johnson's eerie, free-time slide spiritual with moaning vocals that has become a signature slide song for Ry Cooder. This arrangement requires poise in letting go of steady time-keeping, instead playing in relaxed phrases. Tipping the bar in playing both treble and bass melodies, along with some double-string notes, is essential.

"(Sittin' On) The Dock of the Bay" was released after Otis Redding's tragic plane crash and became his most popular original song exactly 50 years before the release of this songbook. Otis wrote with a guitar in open tuning, playing most chords with a finger barring all strings, hence the use of all major chords in this song. Lap slide playing in open D tuning allows you to play the many major chord positions with the steel, while the R&B-style vocal melody is performed on the treble strings in the manner of early blues and slide spirituals. Have patience in learning the tricky bridge section, keeping a slow steady tempo to allow focus on emulating Otis' soulful vocals and whistling!

"Little Martha" is Duane Allman's acoustic fingerpicking showpiece from the *Eat a Peach* album, recorded in tandem with Dickey Betts. To play this piece on lap slide requires learning the single-note melody alone (the first arrangement in the book), then incorporating the open-string alternating bass accompaniment found in the full solo arrangement. For the tune's B section, it's essential to only pick the notated 1st, 2nd, and 4th string chord voicings (avoiding the 3rd string note) to imitate the sound of the Allman's recording more closely. Natural harmonics in the middle and end of the tune are played with the pinky finger of the hand holding the steel.

You Gotta Move

Words and Music by Fred McDowell and Gary Davis

Open D tuning:
(low to high) D-A-D-F#-A-D

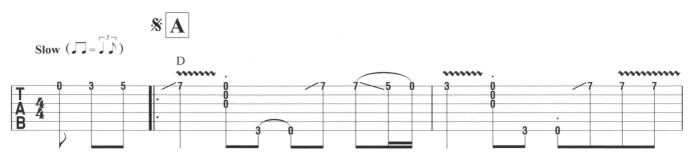

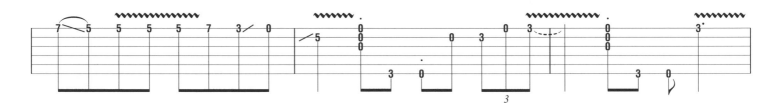

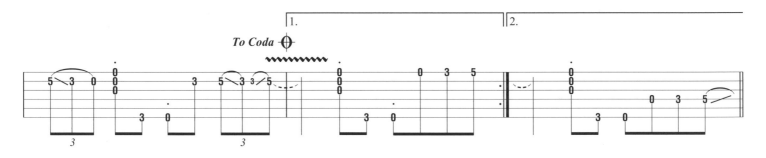

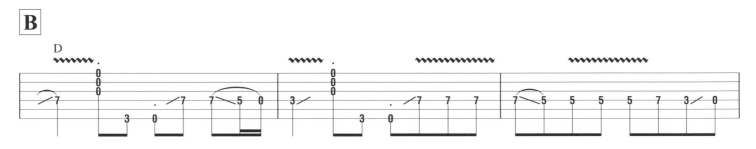

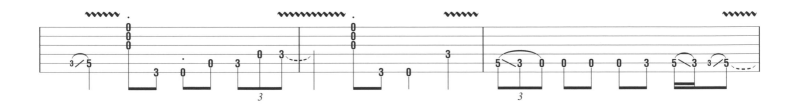

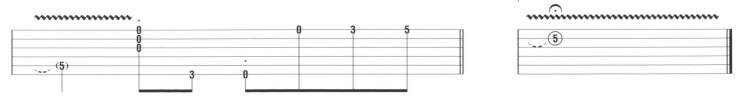

No Expectations

Words and Music by Mick Jagger and Keith Richards

D tuning:
(low to high) D-A-D-F#-A-D

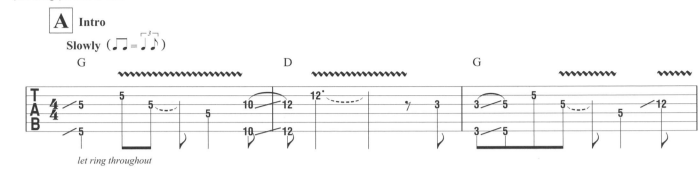

let ring throughout

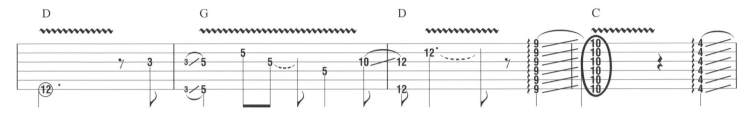

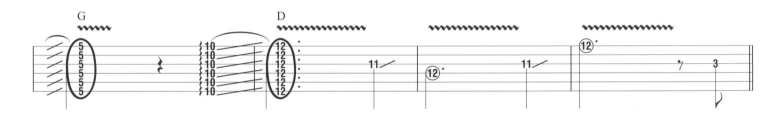

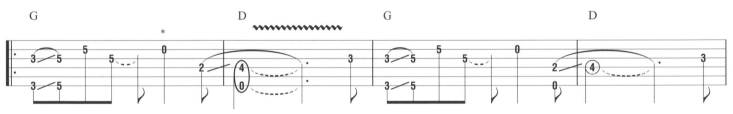

*While sustaining the 5th fret bass note, move bar
off of the 2nd string to achieve open-string note.

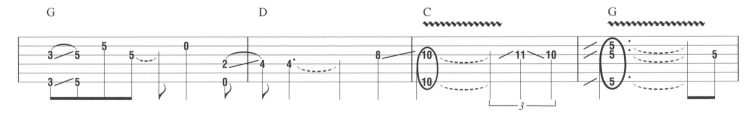

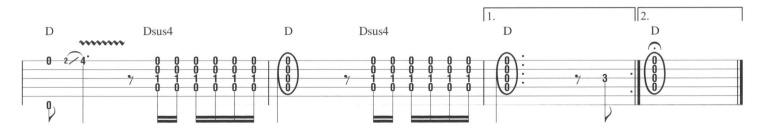

My Babe

Written by Willie Dixon

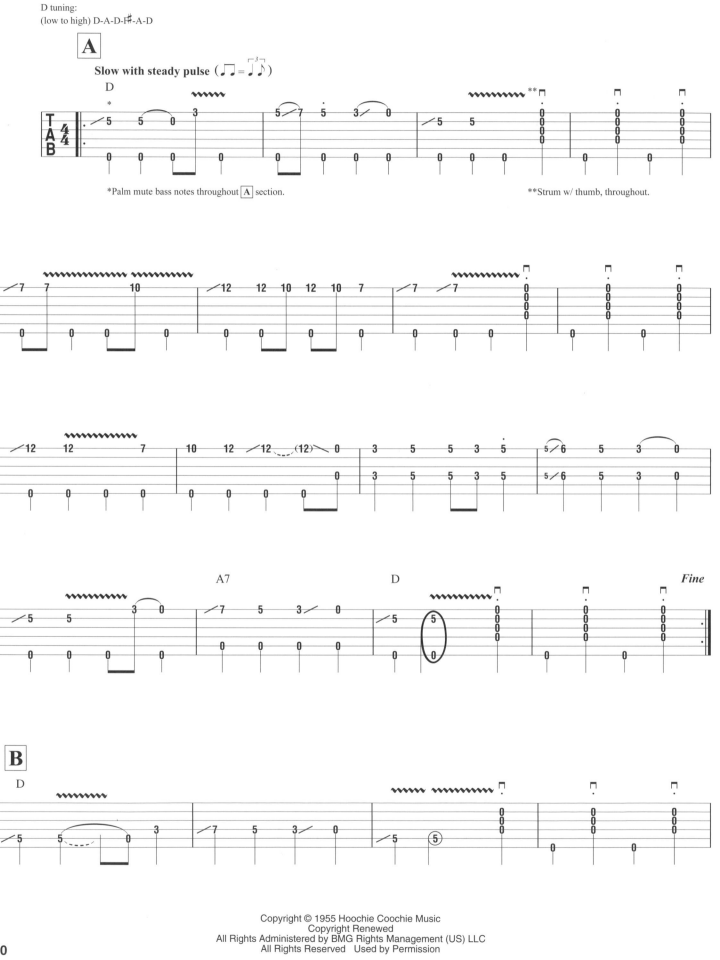

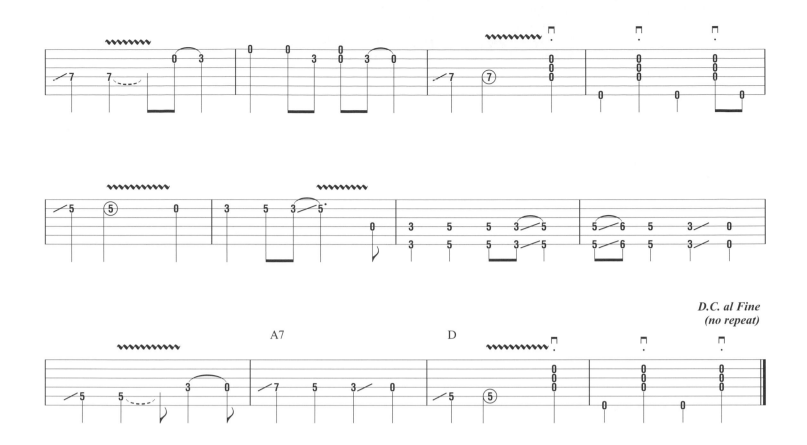

D.C. al Fine
(no repeat)

Outside Woman Blues

Arranged by Eric Clapton

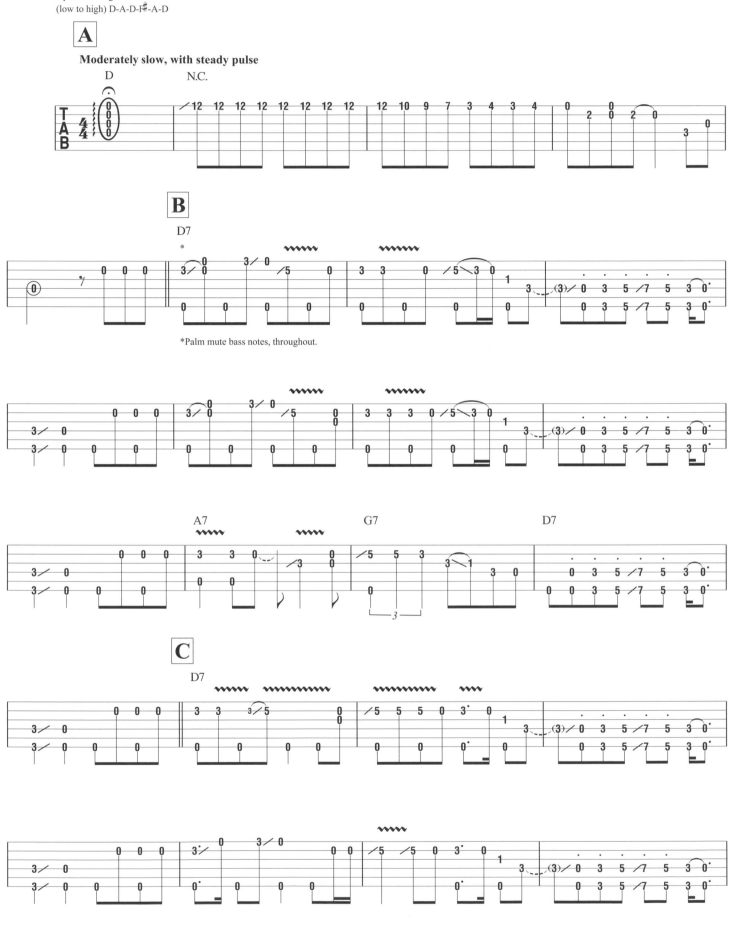

*Palm mute bass notes, throughout.

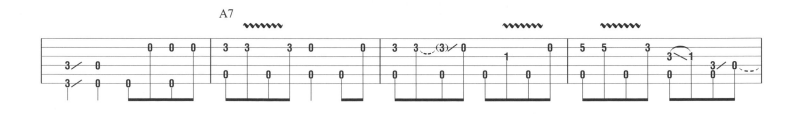

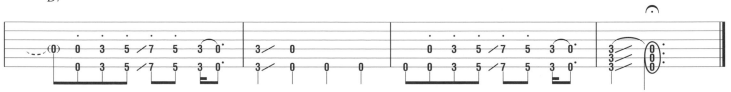

John Henry

West Virginia Folksong

G tuning:
(low to high) D-G-D-G-B-D

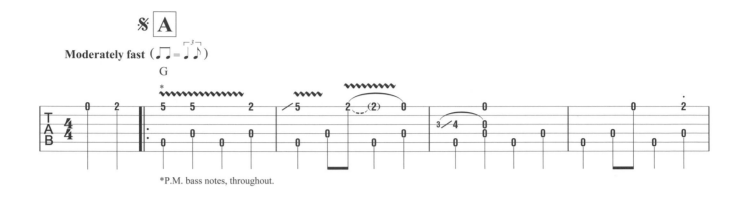

*P.M. bass notes, throughout.

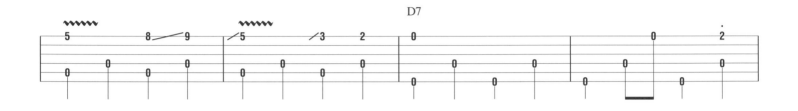

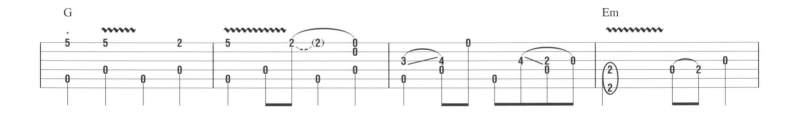

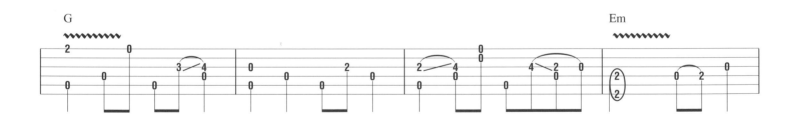

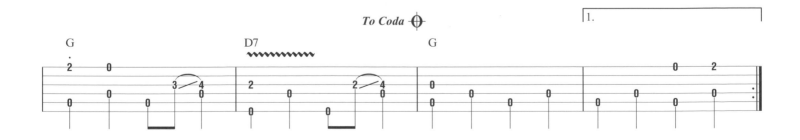

B Solo Break

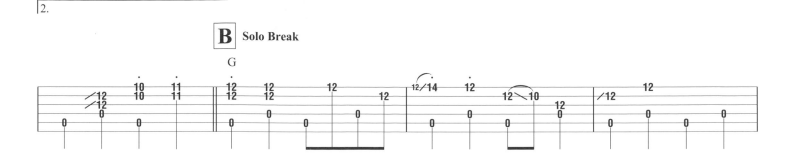

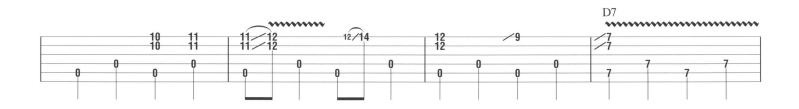

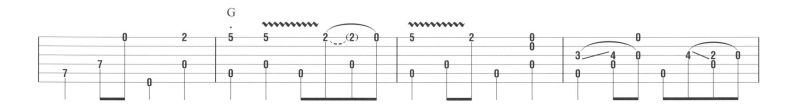

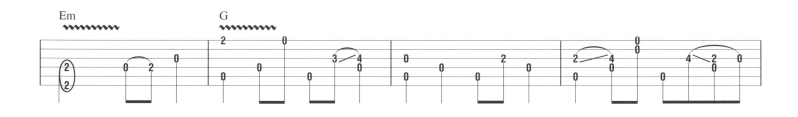

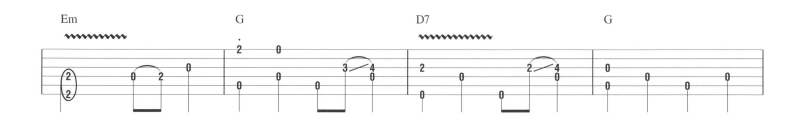

D.S. al Coda   ⊕ **Coda**

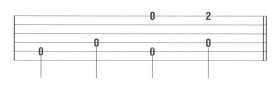

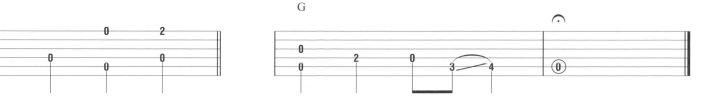

The Soul of a Man

By Blind Willie Johnson

D tuning:
(low to high) D-A-D-F#-A-D

 A

Slow

D7

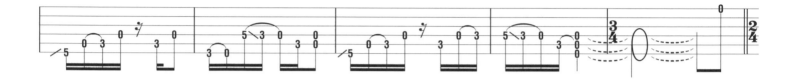

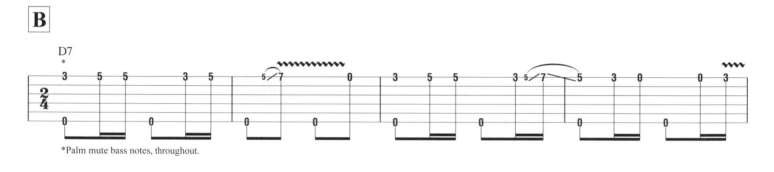

B

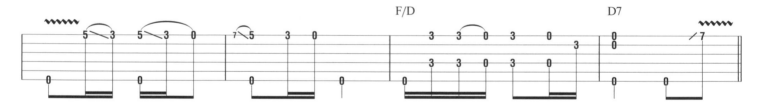

*Palm mute bass notes, throughout.

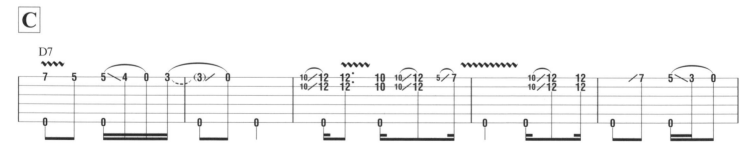

C

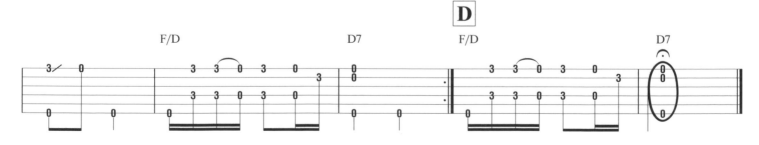

The Great Speckled Bird

Words and Music by Roy Acuff

High-bass G tuning:
(low to high) G-B-D-G-B-D

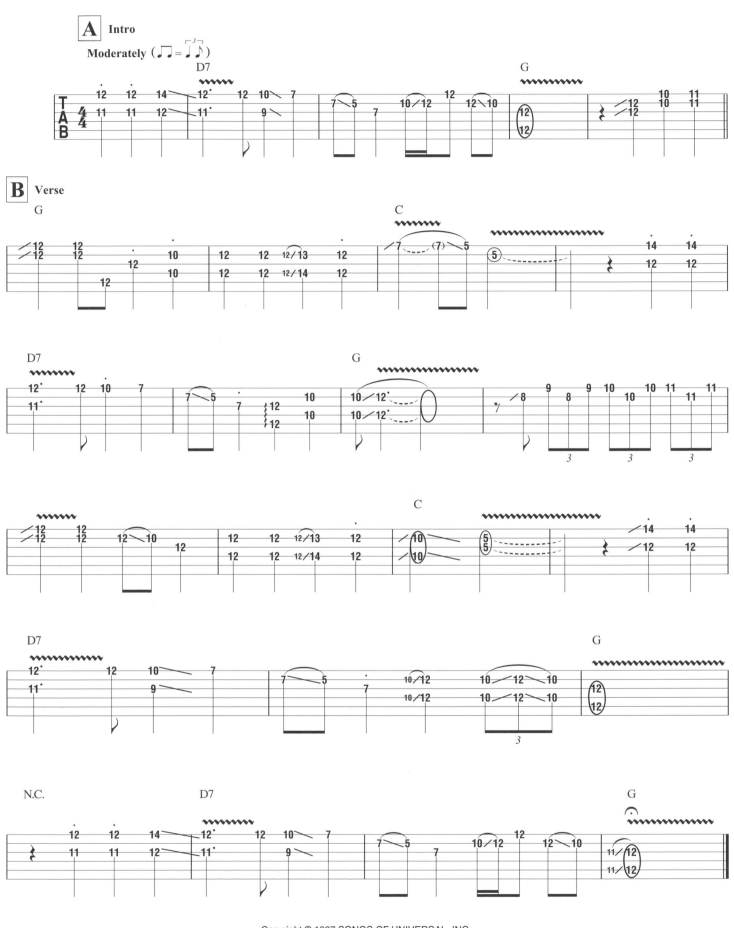

You Are My Sunshine

Words and Music by Jimmie Davis

High-bass G tuning:
(low to high) G-B-D-G-B-D

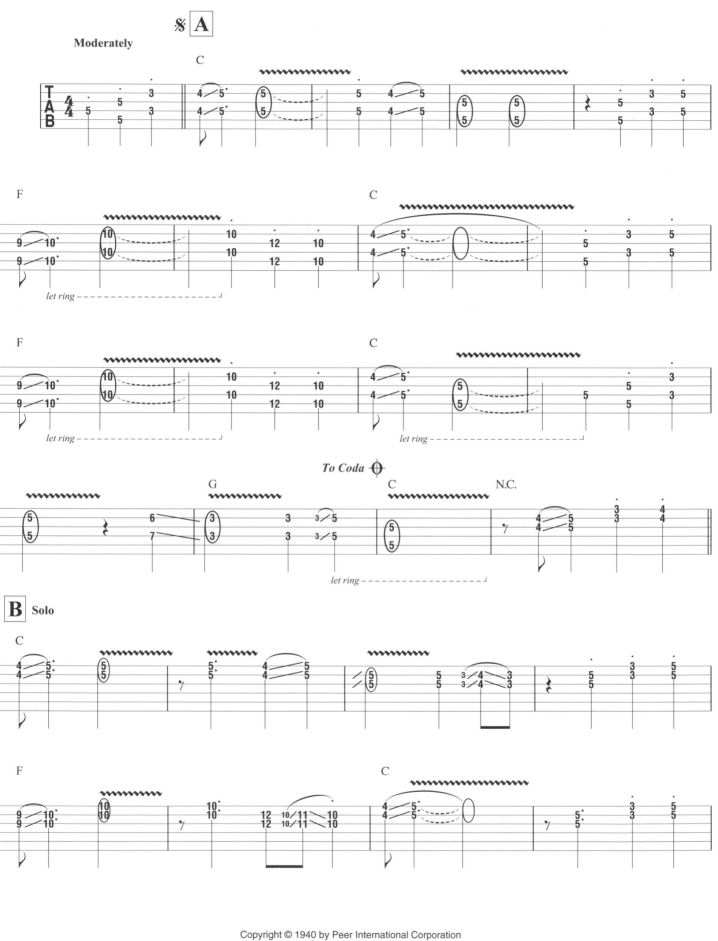

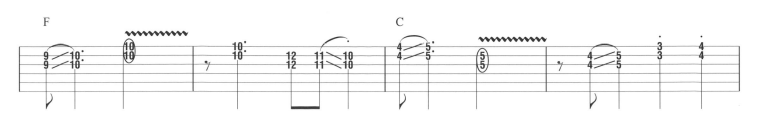

D.S. al Coda

⊕ **Coda**

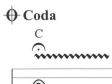
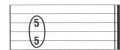

Shenandoah
(Harmony)
American Folksong

High-bass G tuning:
(low to high) G-B-D-G-B-D

Slow, in 2

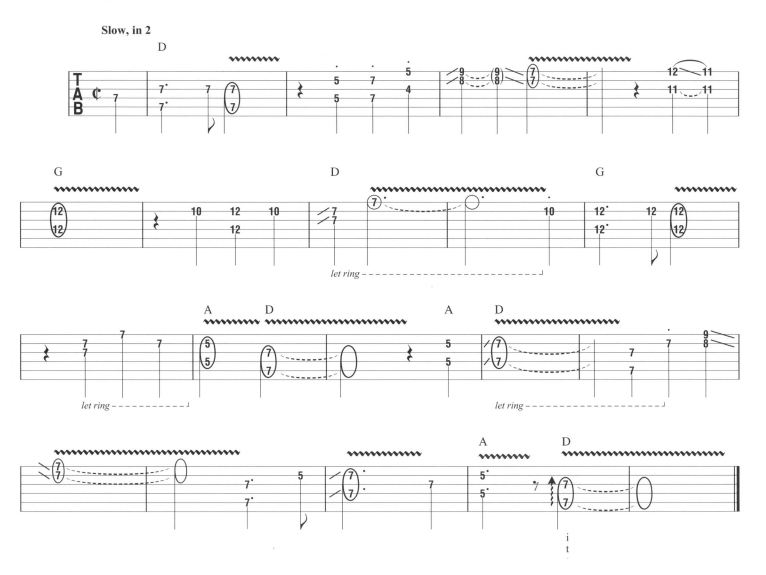

Shenandoah
(Octaves)
American Folksong

High-bass G tuning:
(low to high) G-B-D-G-B-D

Slowly, in 2

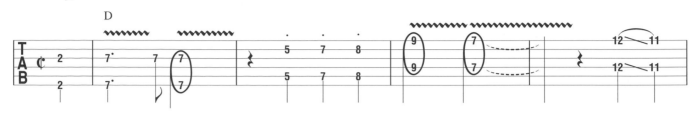

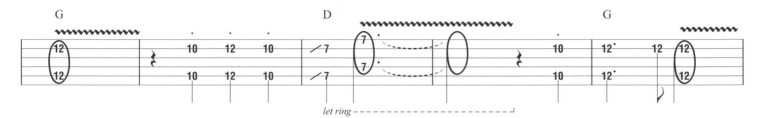

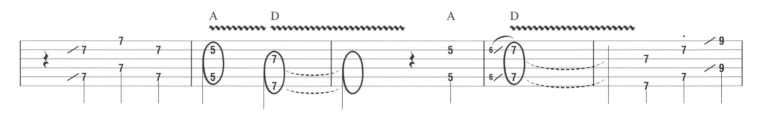

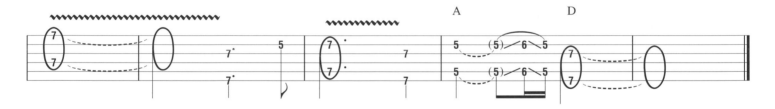

Cripple Creek
(Melody)
American Fiddle Tune

High-bass G tuning:
(low to high) G-B-D-G-B-D

Cripple Creek
(Solo)
American Fiddle Tune

High-bass G tuning:
(low to high) G-B-D-G-B-D

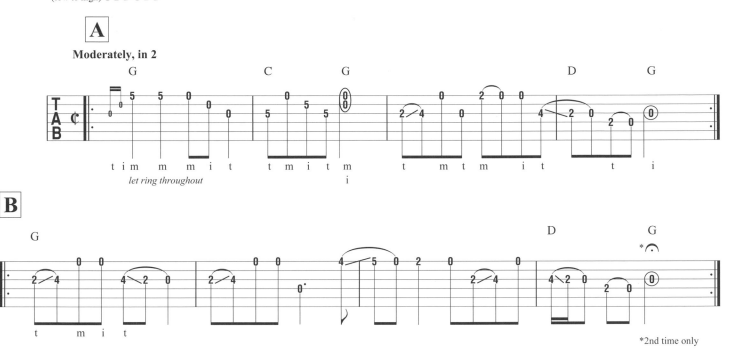

A

Moderately, in 2

B

*2nd time only

Red Wing
(Melody)

Words by Thurland Chattaway
Music by Kerry Mills

High-bass G tuning:
(low to high) G-B-D-G-B-D

Moderately

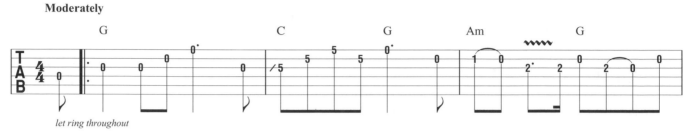

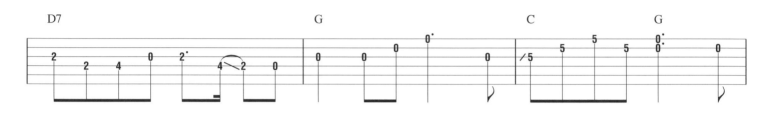

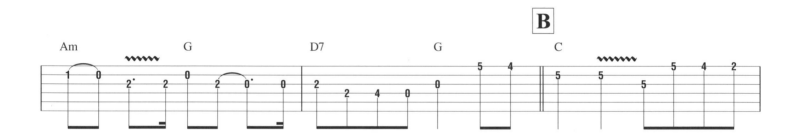

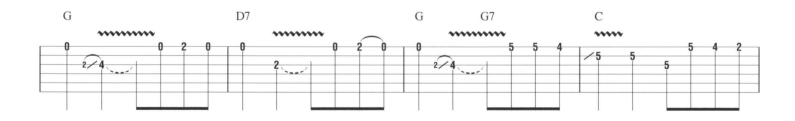

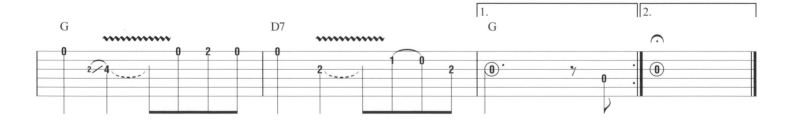

Red Wing
(Solo)

Words by Thurland Chattaway
Music by Kerry Mills

High-bass G tuning:
(low to high) G-B-D-G-B-D

Moderately

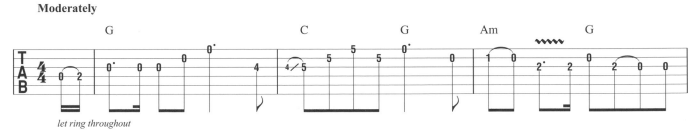

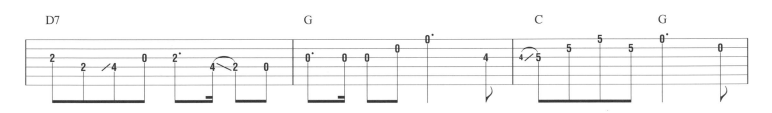

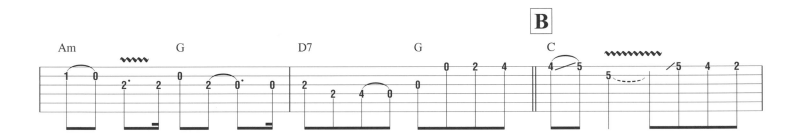

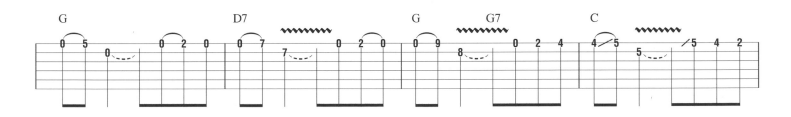

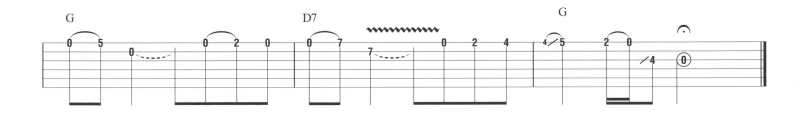

The Red Haired Boy

Old Time Fiddle Tune

High-bass G tuning:
(low to high) G-B-D-G-B-D

A

Moderately, in 2

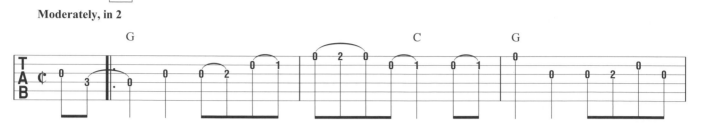

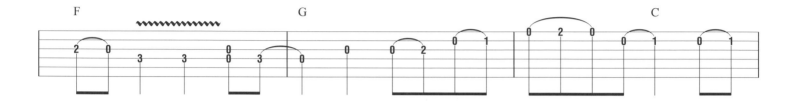

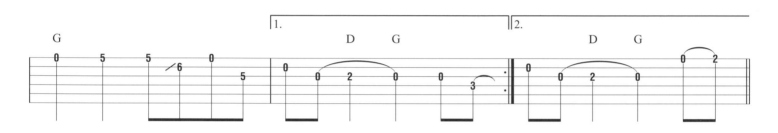

B

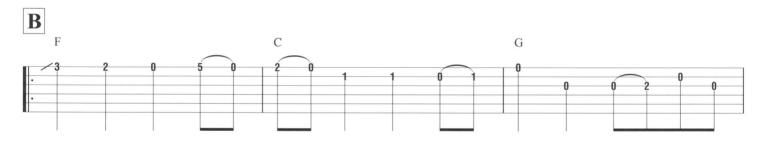

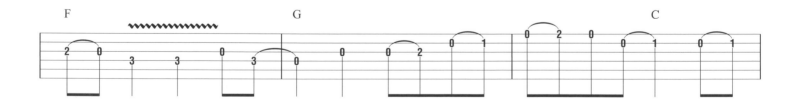

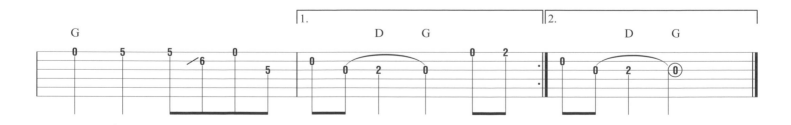

Angelina Baker
(Melody)

Words and Music by Steven Foster

High-bass G tuning:
(low to high) G-B-D-G-B-D

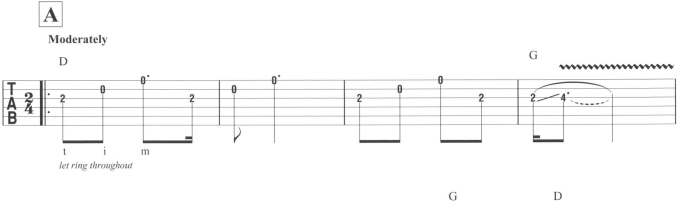

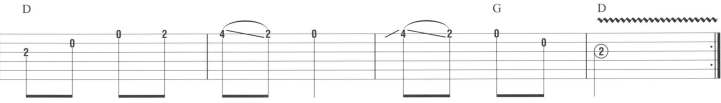

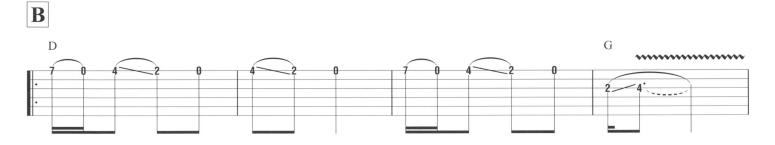

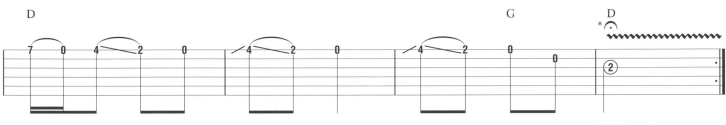

*2nd time only

Angelina Baker
(Harmony)
Words and Music by Steven Foster

High-bass G tuning:
(low to high) G-B-D-G-B-D

Moderately

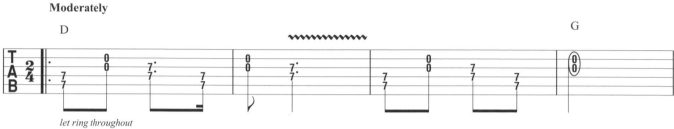

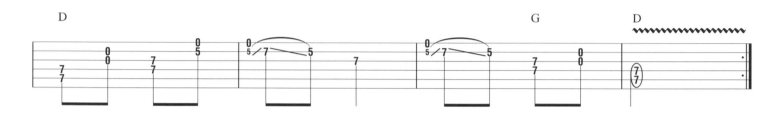

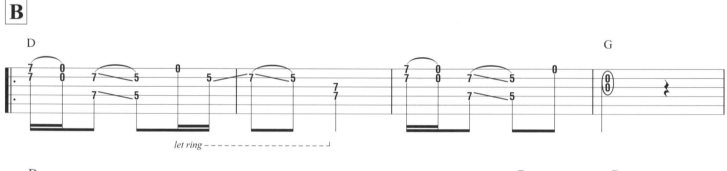

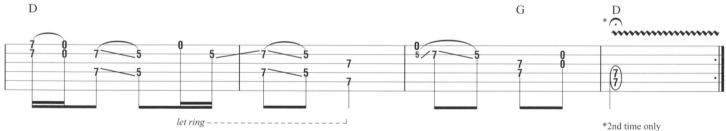

*2nd time only

Lonesome Fiddle Blues

By Vassar Clements

High-bass G tuning:
(low to high) G-B-D-G-B-D

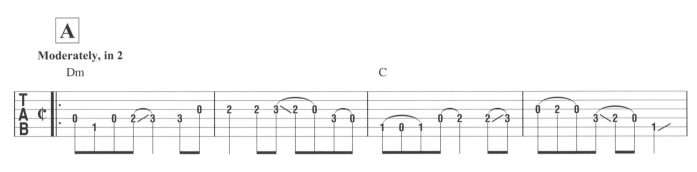

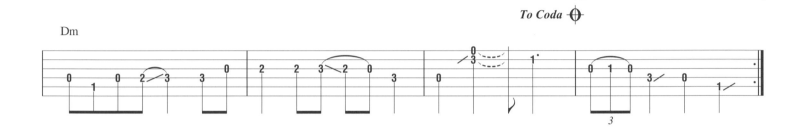

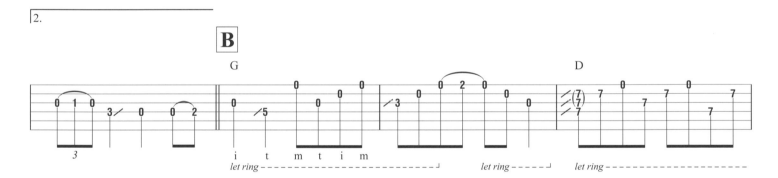

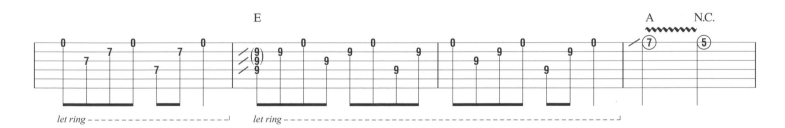

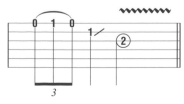

Gold Rush
(Melody)

Words and Music by Bill Monroe

High-bass G tuning:
(low to high) G-B-D-G-B-D

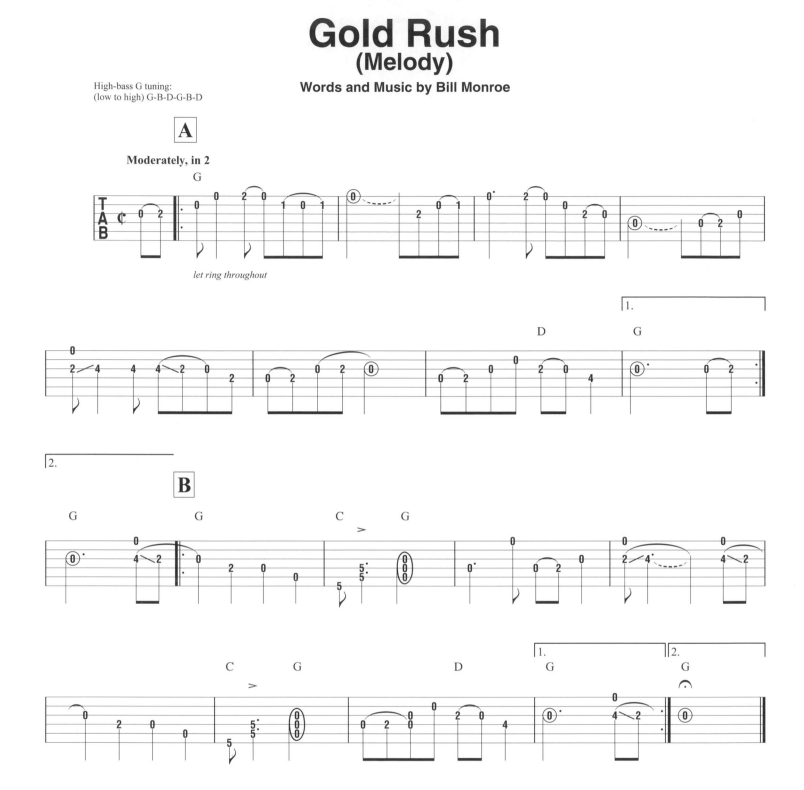

Gold Rush
(Solo)

Words and Music by Bill Monroe

High-bass G tuning:
(low to high) G-B-D-G-B-D

Fireball

Words and Music by Lester Flatt, Burkett Graves and Earl Scruggs

High-bass G tuning:
(low to high) G-B-D-G-B-D

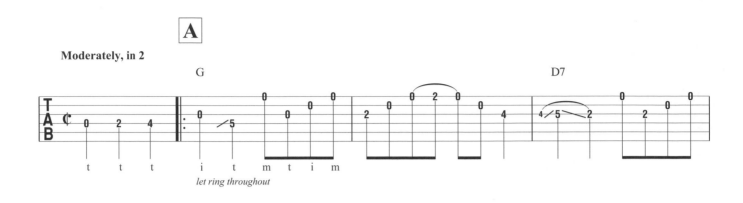

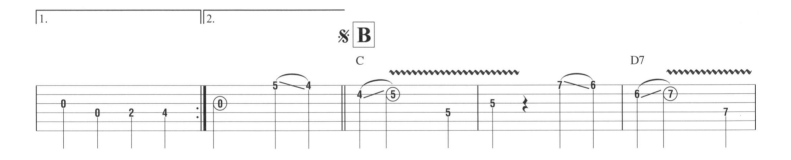

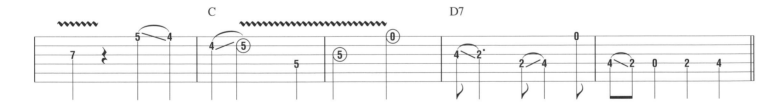

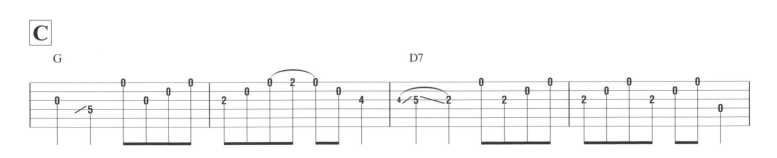

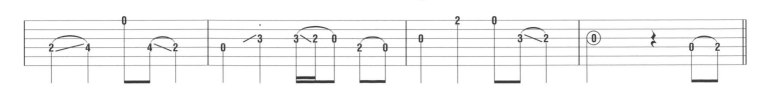

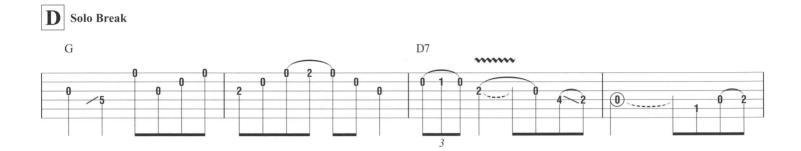

D Solo Break

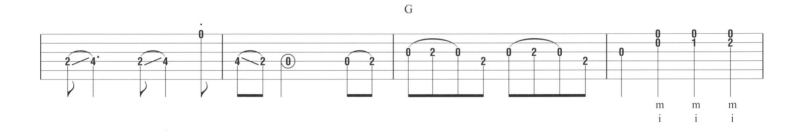

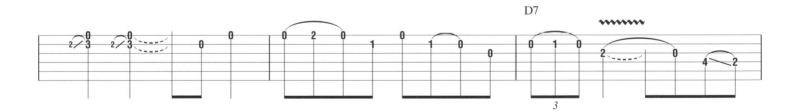

D.S. al Coda   **Coda**

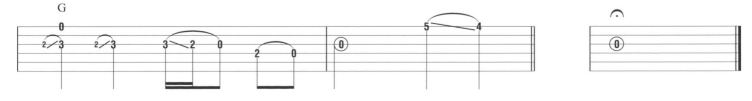

Poor Boy, Long Ways from Home

Traditional

G tuning:
(low to high) D-G-D-G-B-D

A Intro Solo

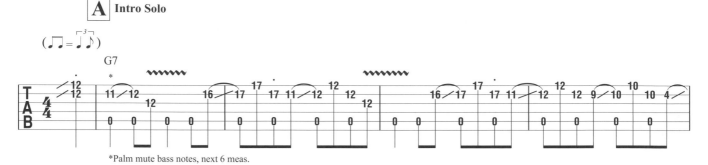

*Palm mute bass notes, next 6 meas.

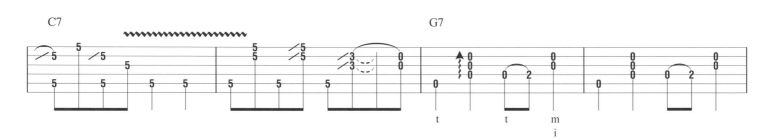

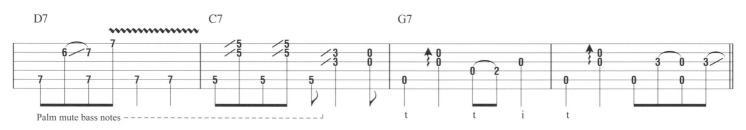

Palm mute bass notes - - - - - - - - - - - - - -

B Verse Melody

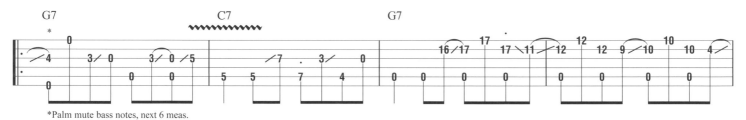

*Palm mute bass notes, next 6 meas.

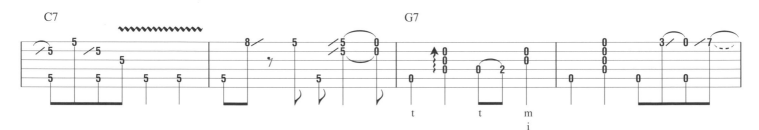

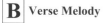

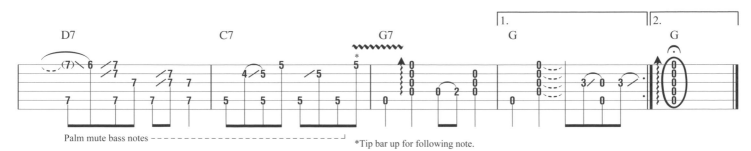

Palm mute bass notes -   *Tip bar up for following note.

Steamboat Gwine 'Round de Bend

Written by John Fahey

G tuning:
(low to high) D-G-D-G-B-D

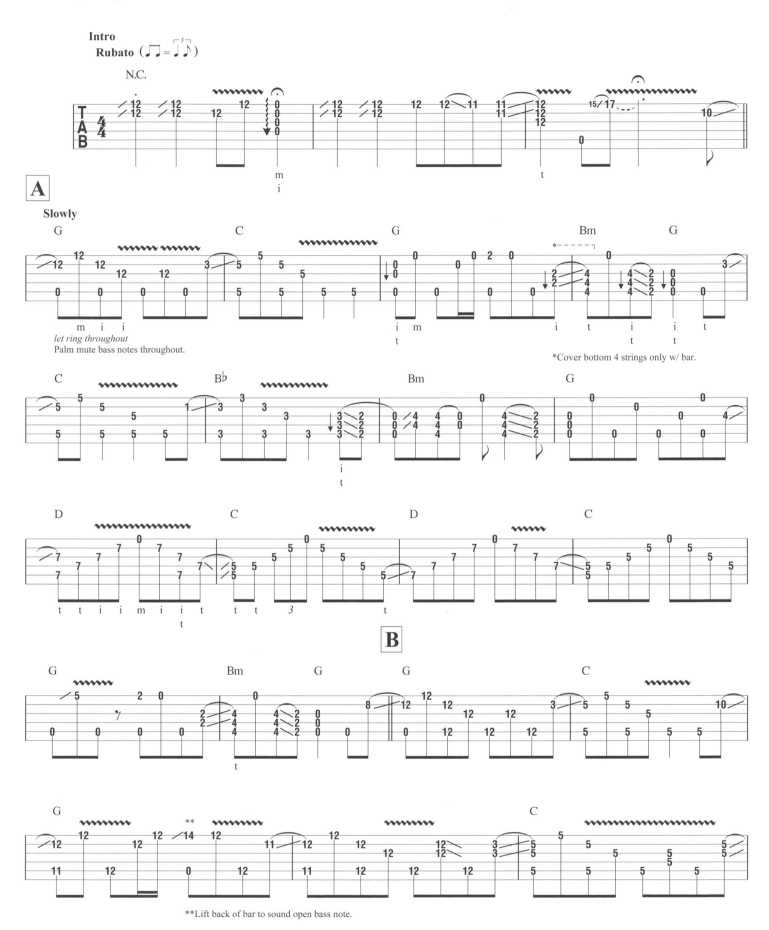

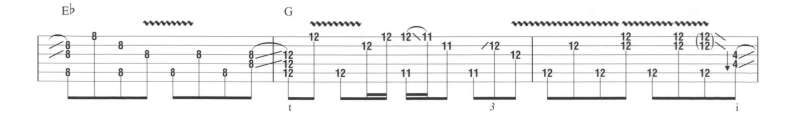

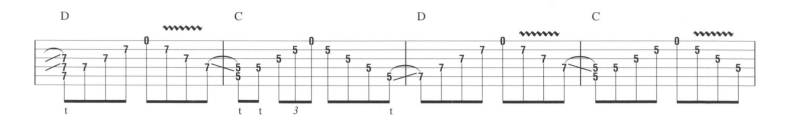

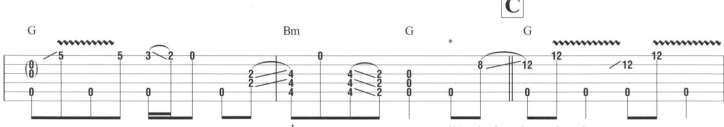

C

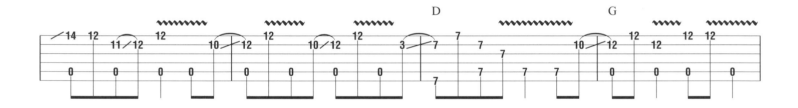

*Move bar forward to sound open bass.

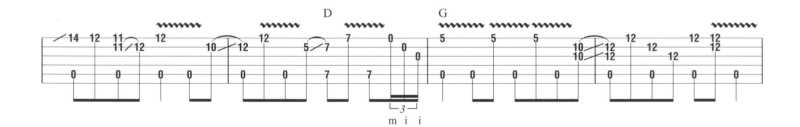

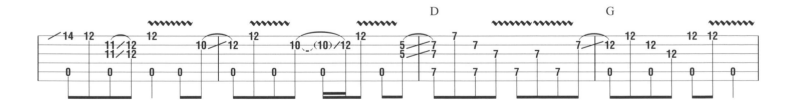

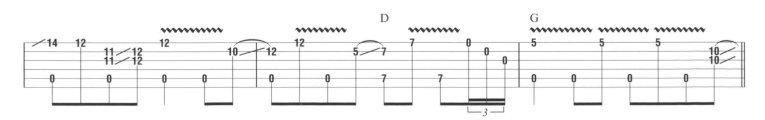

D

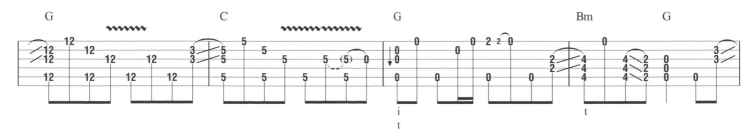

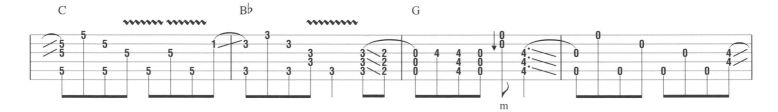

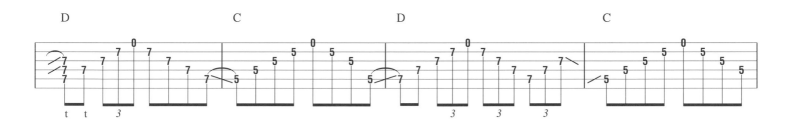

E

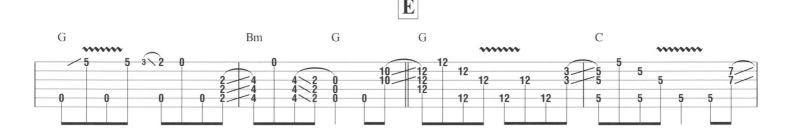

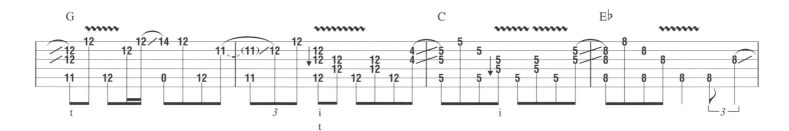

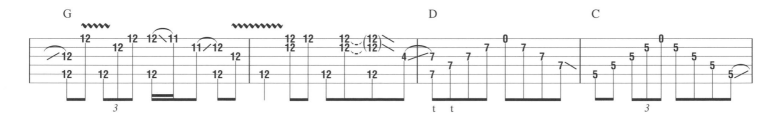

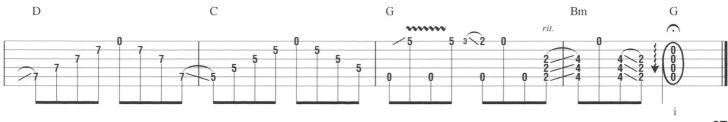

Come on in My Kitchen

Words and Music by Robert Johnson

G tuning:
(low to high) D-G-D-G-B-D

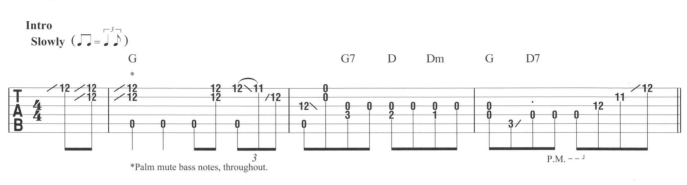

*Palm mute bass notes, throughout.

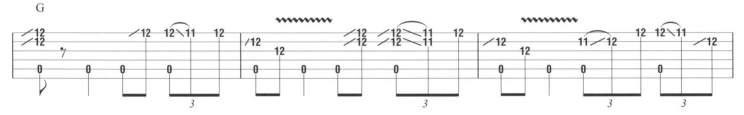

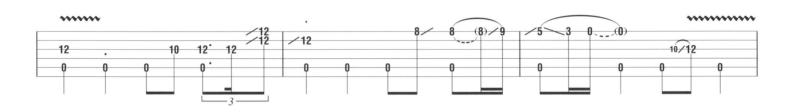

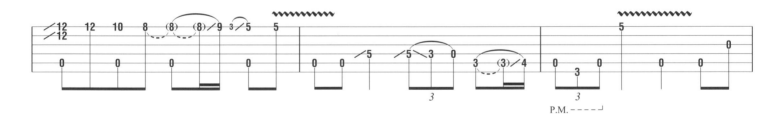

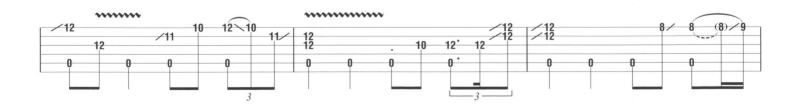

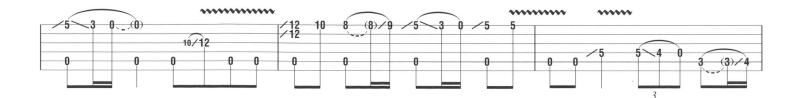

Bridge

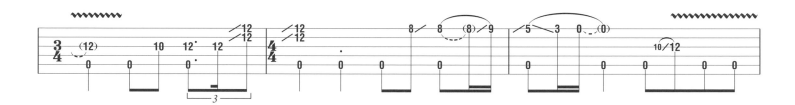

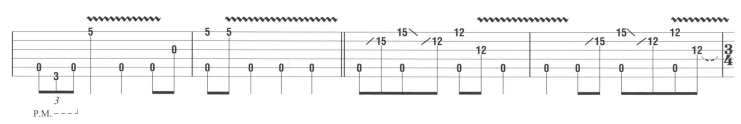

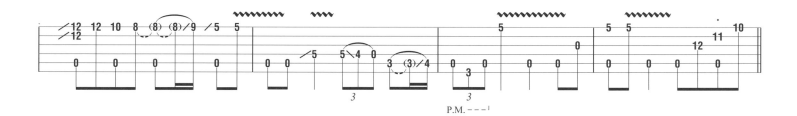

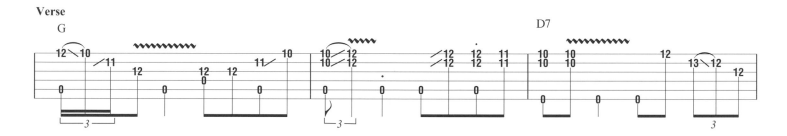

Verse

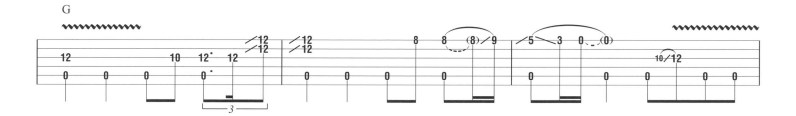

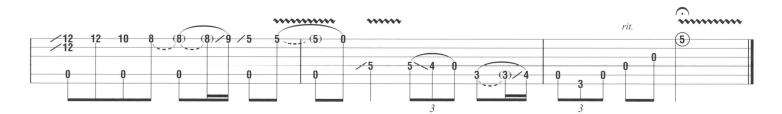

Dark Was the Night, Cold Was the Ground

Words and Music by Blind Willie Johnson

Open D tuning:
(low to high) D-A-D-F#-A-D

Slowly
Rubato

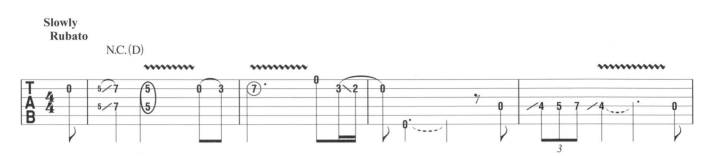

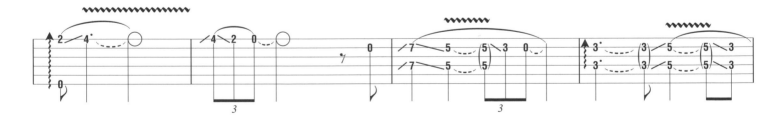

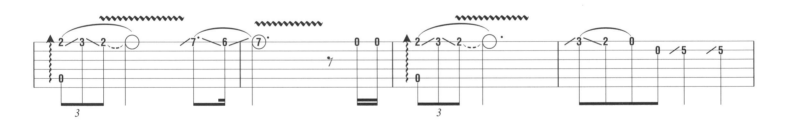

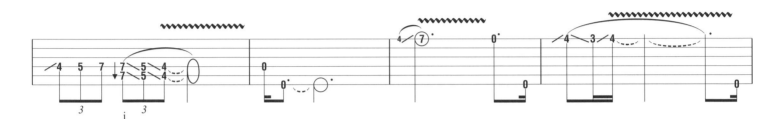

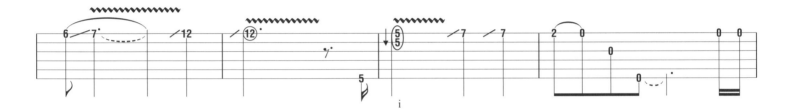

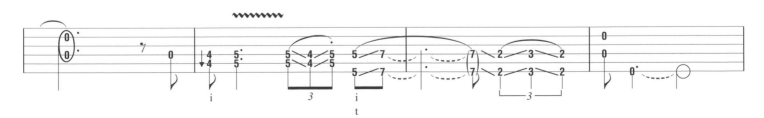

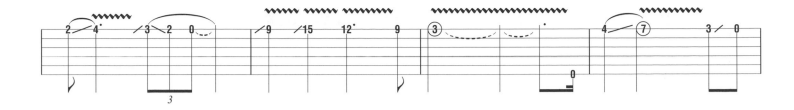

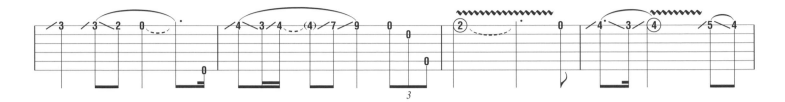

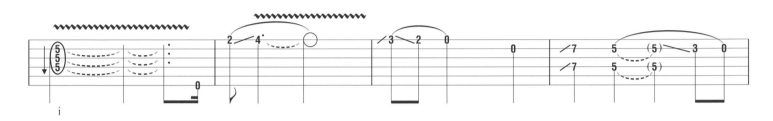

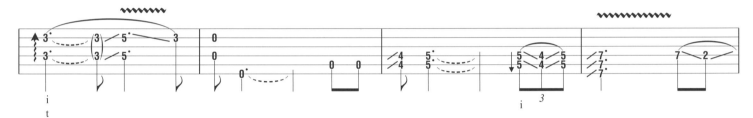

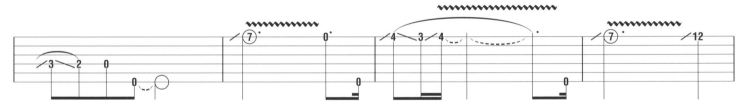

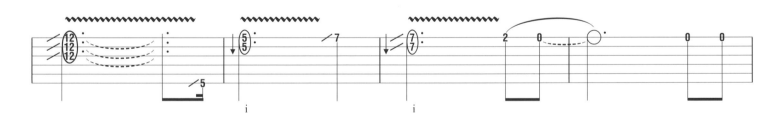

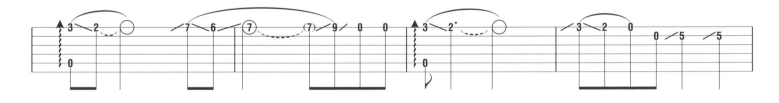

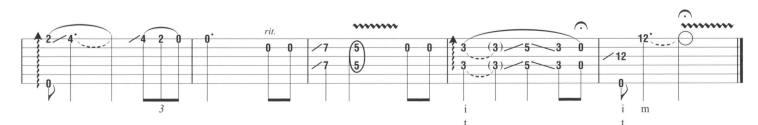

(Sittin' On) The Dock of the Bay

Words and Music by Steve Cropper and Otis Redding

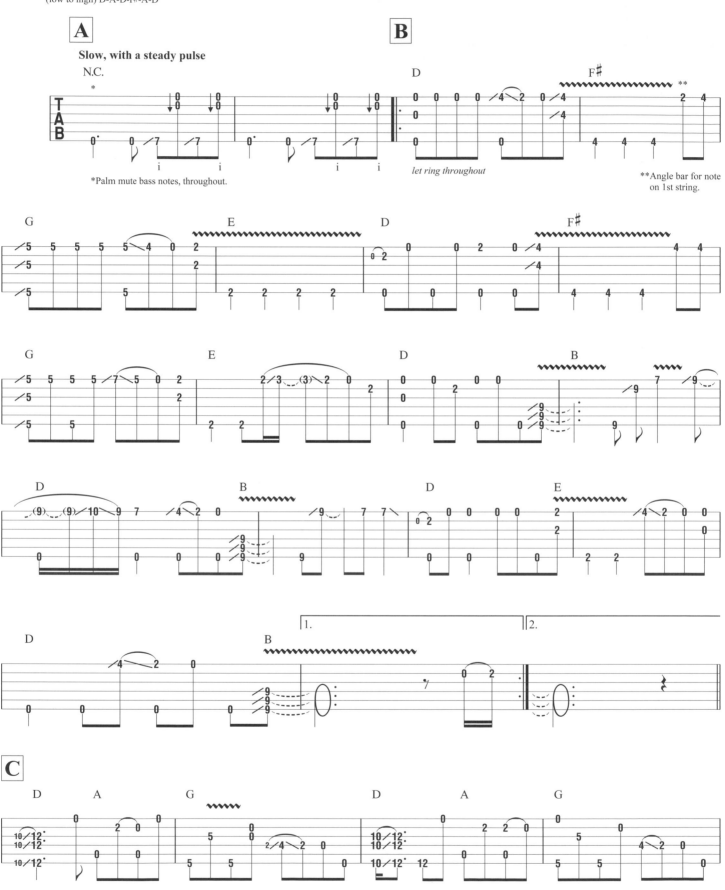

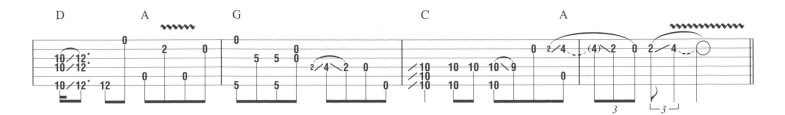

 D

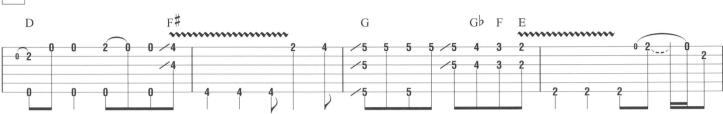

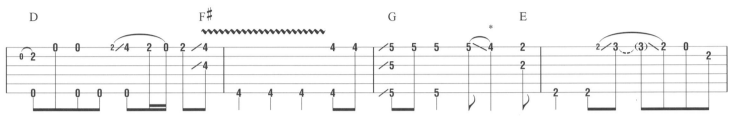

*Angle bar, as before (till end, where indicated).

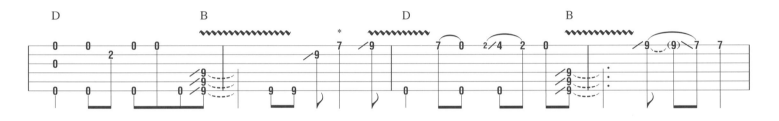

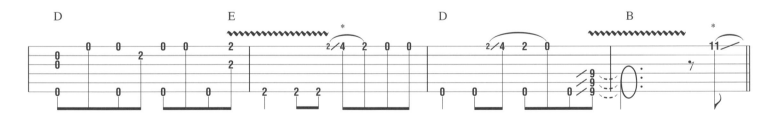

E

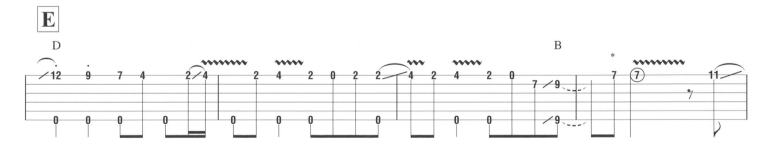

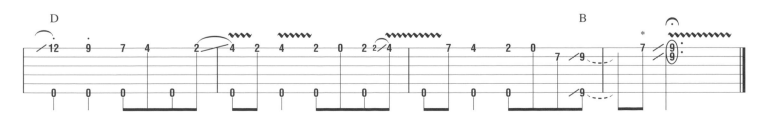

Little Martha
(Solo)
By Duane Allman

Open D tuning:
(low to high) D-A-D-F#-A-D

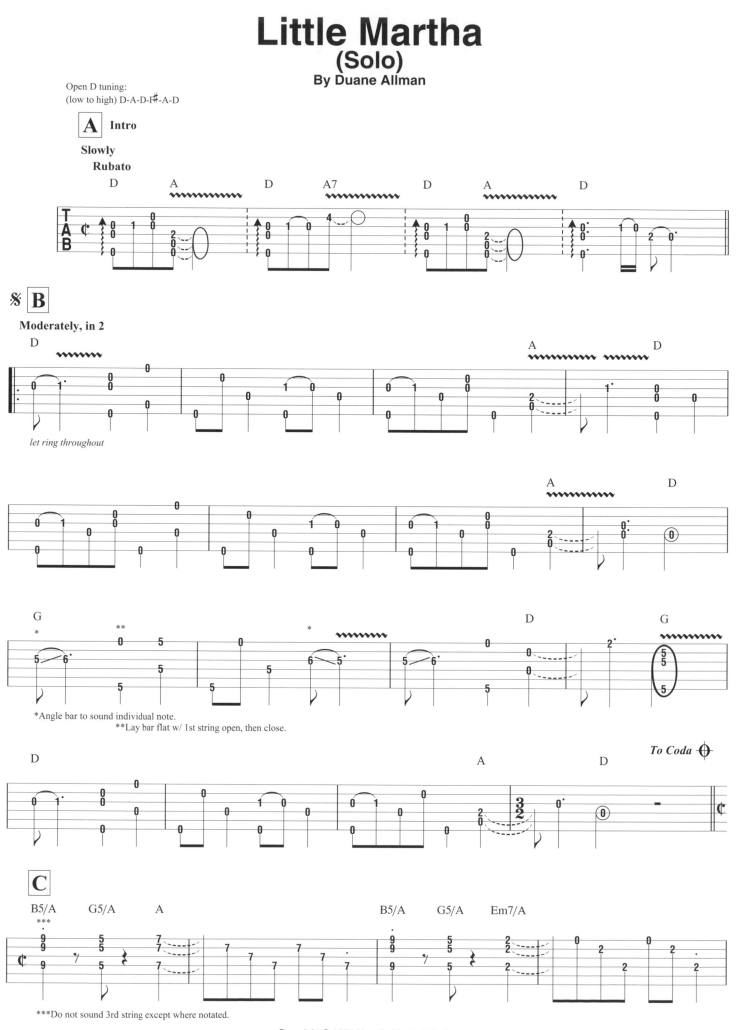

*Angle bar to sound individual note.
**Lay bar flat w/ 1st string open, then close.

***Do not sound 3rd string except where notated.

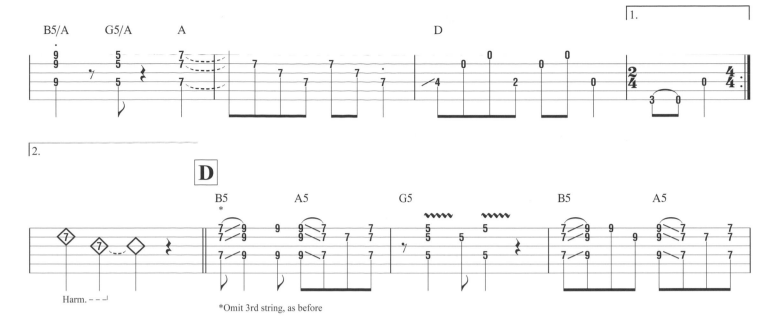

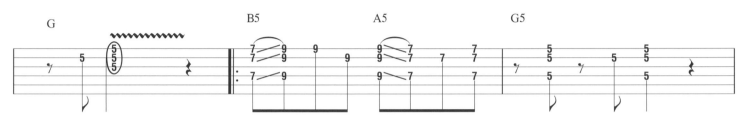

*Omit 3rd string, as before

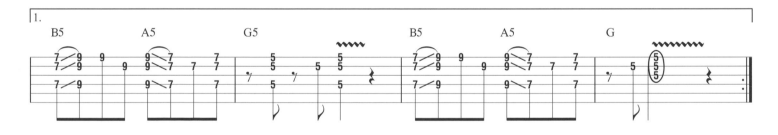

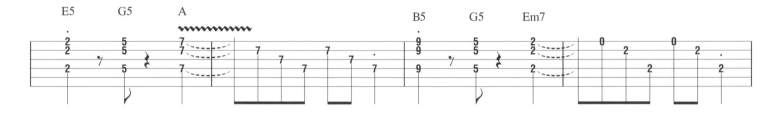

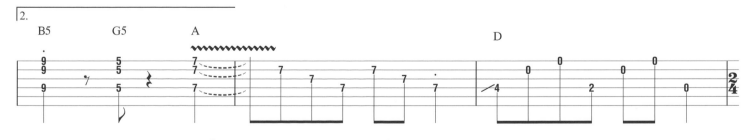

Coda

Rubato

D.S. al Coda

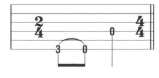

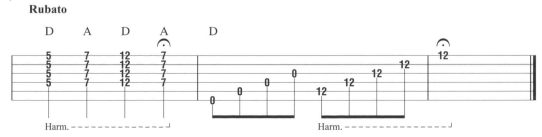

Little Martha
(Melody)
By Duane Allman

D tuning:
(low to high) D-A-D-F#-A-D

A

Moderately, in 2

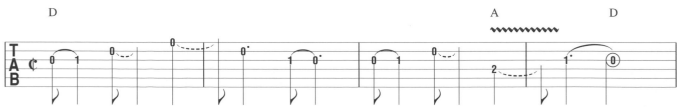

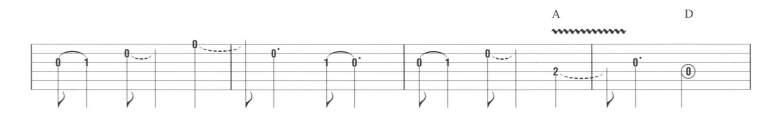

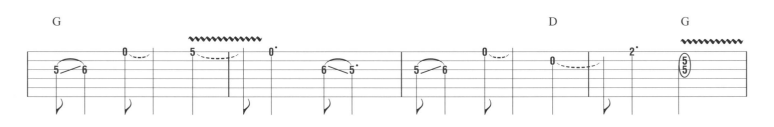

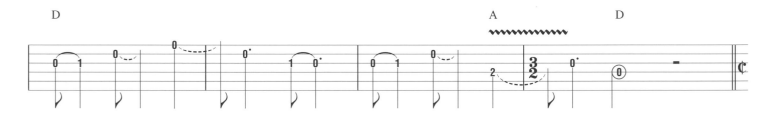

B

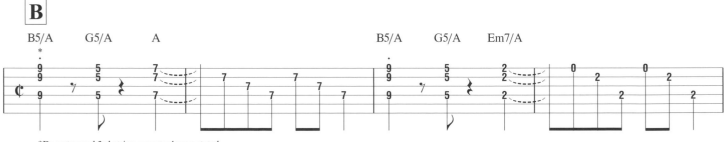

*Do not sound 3rd string except where notated.

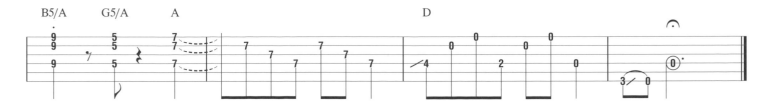

LAP SLIDE RHYTHM TAB LEGEND

Rhythm Tab is a form of notation that adds rhythmic values to the traditional tab staff.

TABLATURE graphically represents the guitar fretboard. Each horizontal line represents a string, and each number represents a fret. Rhythmic values are shown using ovals, stems, and dots.

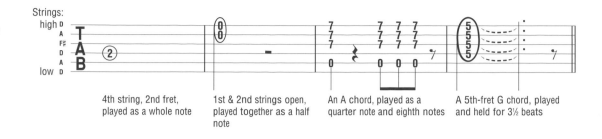

4th string, 2nd fret, played as a whole note

1st & 2nd strings open, played together as a half note

An A chord, played as a quarter note and eighth notes

A 5th-fret G chord, played and held for 3½ beats

Definitions for Special Guitar Notation

LEGATO SLIDE: Strike the first note and then slide up or down to the second note. The second note is not struck.

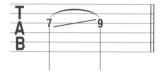

SHIFT SLIDE: Same as legato slide, except the second note is struck.

GRACE NOTE SLIDE: Quickly slide into the note from below or above.

VIBRATO: The note is vibrated by rapidly sliding the bar back and forth along the string.

HAMMER-ON: Strike the first note, then sound the higher note (on the same string) with the slide bar by fretting it without picking.

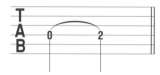

PULL-OFF: Strike the first note, then pull the slide bar off to sound the second (lower) note without picking.

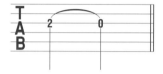

MUFFLED STRINGS: A percussive sound is produced by laying the fret hand across the string(s) without depressing, and striking them with the pick hand.

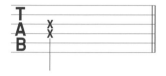

NATURAL HARMONIC: Strike the note while the fret-hand lightly touches the string directly over the fret indicated.

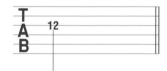

Harm.

ARPEGGIATE: Play the notes of the chord indicated by quickly rolling them from bottom to top.

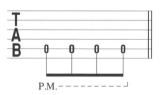

PALM MUTING: The note is partially muted by the pick hand lightly touching the string(s) just before the bridge.

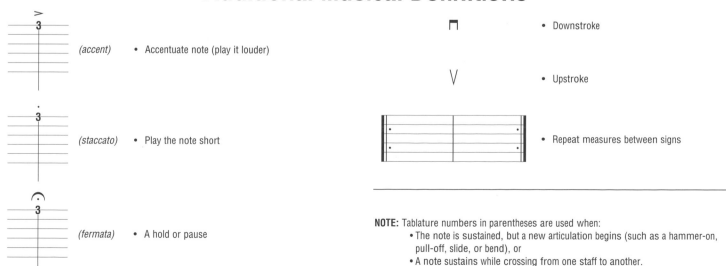

P.M.

Additional Musical Definitions

(accent) • Accentuate note (play it louder)

(staccato) • Play the note short

(fermata) • A hold or pause

⊓ • Downstroke

∨ • Upstroke

• Repeat measures between signs

NOTE: Tablature numbers in parentheses are used when:
• The note is sustained, but a new articulation begins (such as a hammer-on, pull-off, slide, or bend), or
• A note sustains while crossing from one staff to another.